> "THERE IS NO PERFECT BEAUTY THAT HATH NOT STRANGENESS IN THE PROPORTION"
>
> Francis Bacon, London 1639

OUTBACK
PRINT

First published in Australia 2000

OUTBACK
P R I N T

2/98 Spit Road, Mosman NSW Australia

ISBN 0 949155 31 4

Copyright © Australia museum
Outback Print

CONTENTS

THE BEAUTIFUL IMAGES AND TEXTS YOU SEE IN THIS BOOK COME FROM THE AUSTRALIAN MUSEUM'S BODY ART EXHIBITION. THIS EXHIBITION, TWO YEARS IN THE MAKING, WAS CREATED BY A DEDICATED GROUP OF STAFF FROM THE AUSTRALIAN MUSEUM WITH THE VERY GENEROUS INPUT OF OVER 100 PEOPLE FROM A RANGE OF COMMUNITIES WHO PRACTICE DIFFERENT FORMS OF BODY ART.

THE AUSTRALIAN MUSEUM GREATLY APPRECIATES THE ASSISTANCE OF TELSTRA, THE SPONSOR OF BODY ART AND FLASH PHOTOBITION AUSTRALIA, A GENEROUS SUPPORTER OF THIS EXHIBITION.

THANKS MUST GO TO THE STAFF ON THE PROJECT TEAM FOR THEIR FANTASTIC EFFORTS IN DEVELOPING THE EXHIBITION: SUE ANDERSON, JEANNINE BAKER, LEANNE BRASS, KATINKA CARR, YVONNE CARRILLO, PETER KLOBE, LEONÉ LEMMER, TRISH MCDONALD, TIKI RAND, LINDA RAYMOND, ADRIENNE RICHARDS, JULIE TURNER AND CHERYLE YIN-LO. THANKS TO OTHER STAFF PARTICIPANTS IN THE PROJECT TEAM: PAUL TAÇON, LAINA DE WINNE, DANYELLE DROGA, ANNE LECULIER AND COLIN MACGREGOR.

SPECIAL THANKS GO TO CARL BENTO, PAUL OVENDEN, STUART HUMPHREYS AND JAMES KING IN THE PHOTOGRAPHY UNIT FOR THE INCREDIBLE AMOUNT OF WORK THEY PUT IN, SEVEN DAYS A WEEK, TO CREATE THESE GORGEOUS IMAGES. AND TO TIKI (KRISTINA) RAND, WHO MANIPULATED THESE IMAGES AND CREATED THESE BEAUTIFUL COMBINATIONS OF TEXT AND GRAPHICS, CONGRATULATIONS ON A JOB WELL DONE.

WITHOUT EACH AND EVERY PARTICIPANT GIVING SO MUCH OF THEIR TIME – TELLING THEIR STORIES, BEING PHOTOGRAPHED, LENDING OBJECTS AND GIVING ADVICE AND INFORMATION – BODY ART WOULD NOT HAVE REALISED ITS POTENTIAL AS AN ENGAGING, CONFRONTING AND FASCINATING EXPERIENCE. WE ARE ENORMOUSLY GRATEFUL TO ALL.

IN PARTICULAR, THE AUSTRALIAN MUSEUM WISHES TO ESPECIALLY ACKNOWLEDGE AND THANK THE PEOPLE WHOSE BODIES AND ART ADORN THIS BOOK.

ENJOY THIS BOOK THAT CELEBRATES THE DIVERSITY, BEAUTY, IMPORTANCE AND RELEVANCE OF BODY ART.

PROFESSOR MICHAEL ARCHER
DIRECTOR, AUSTRALIAN MUSEUM

BODY ART: A PERSONAL AFFAIR, AN ANCIENT TRADITION

FEW THINGS ARE MORE INTIMATE, MORE PERSONAL AND MORE SPECIAL THAN OUR BODIES. EACH OF US EXPRESSES THIS CLOSE RELATIONSHIP TO OUR BODIES IN UNIQUE AND VARIED WAYS. FOR PERHAPS HUNDREDS OF THOUSANDS OF YEARS, WE HAVE DECORATED, ADORNED, MARKED AND MODIFIED OUR PHYSICAL SELVES IN PLAIN, ELABORATE AND OUTRAGEOUS WAYS. IN THE PROCESS, WE HAVE ILLUSTRATED, REAFFIRMED AND EXPRESSED ANEW WHAT IT MEANS TO BE HUMAN. HUMANS NOT ONLY MAKE TOOLS, USE LANGUAGE, CREATE 'ART' AND MODIFY LANDSCAPES, BUT ALSO ENHANCE THEIR OWN NATURAL FEATURES IN THE PROCESS OF EXHIBITING WHO AND WHAT THEY ARE. INDEED, HOMO SAPIENS CAN BE DEFINED AS THE CREATURE THAT CONTINUALLY TRANSFORMS ITSELF, AS WELL AS THE WORLD AROUND IT.

When did this obsession with our bodies begin? Why did we paint, clothe, pierce, scar, tattoo, shape and adorn our bodies in the first place? Why not roam the world naked? After all, that is what other creatures do. How did body art become so varied, take on so many forms and, in some cases, become so time and labour intensive?

FIRST OF ALL, BODY ART KNOWS NO BOUNDS OTHER THAN THE HUMAN IMAGINATION. BODY ART IS ABOUT IDENTITY, CONTROL AND COMMUNICATION. IT IS ABOUT STATUS, INITIATION AND RITES OF PASSAGE. IT IS ABOUT SEX AND BEING SEXY. IT ALSO IS ABOUT OBSCURING, MASKING, CHANGING AND TRANSFORMING. BUT ABOVE ALL ELSE, BODY ART IS ABOUT OURSELVES — WHO WE ARE, WHERE WE HAVE COME FROM, HOW WE FEEL, WHERE WE ARE GOING. IT IS ABOUT MAKING STATEMENTS TO BOTH OTHERS AND OURSELVES. IN THIS SENSE, IT CAN BE BOTH LITERALLY AND FIGURATIVELY DEEPLY PERSONAL BUT IT USUALLY ALSO REFLECTS GROUP CONCERNS, SOCIETIES, NATIONS AND EVEN INTERNATIONAL TRENDS. AS A RESULT, BODY ART GIVES US A FASCINATING GLIMPSE INTO THE HEART OF BOTH PEOPLE AND PLACES, REVEALING CULTURAL NORMS, HIDDEN SECRETS AND PERSONAL TASTES, AS WELL AS SPONTANEITY, CREATIVITY AND CHANGING SENSES OF AESTHETICS.

Body art may have initially been triggered by a very early attraction to bright and colourful objects, as well as a typically human preoccupation with sex. From an evolutionary perspective, this likely occurred some time after humans began to walk on two feet, about 4-6 million years ago. One of the consequences of upright posture was a change in orientation and shape of the pelvis, with female reproductive organs more hidden. Buttocks became less obvious and there was a change from the back to the front in terms of sexual signalling and attraction, for both males and females. Many anthropologists believe female breasts replaced the buttocks as a sexual lure at this time and that breast size increased as males mated with females with these increasingly exaggerated features. At the same time, the penis became larger and more prominent for display, again as a result of mating. Breasts with less hair may have been particularly enticing, perhaps signalling youthfulness and vigour. It is believed that, increasingly, hairlessness was selected for by both sexes. Bare skin, previously confined to buttocks, become a sexy feature in terms of choosing a mate. But as soon as we became naked, it seems that we wanted to cover up, with clothing, paint, objects and all manner of mark.

WALKING UPRIGHT ALSO FREED THE HANDS FOR NEW POSSIBILITIES OF TOOL MANUFACTURE, COMMUNICATION AND THE EXPLORATION OF BODIES. IT AFFECTED THE TORSO, ALLOWING THE LUNGS AND DIAPHRAGM TO MAKE MORE COMPLEX SOUNDS. ENGLISH ARCHAEOLOGIST TIMOTHY TAYLOR (1996:6-7) BELIEVES LANGUAGE DEVELOPED ABOUT 1.6 MILLION YEARS AGO, WITH THE HUMAN ANCESTOR HOMO ERECTUS, 'AND WITH IT THE FIRST DECLARATIONS OF LOVE, BOTH SINCERE AND INSINCERE'. HE ALSO BELIEVES THE FIRST CLOTHING WAS LIKELY TO HAVE BEEN INVENTED AT THIS TIME, PERHAPS TO 'CONCEAL OR ENHANCE THE GENITAL REGION AND THEREFORE EXTEND CONSCIOUS CONTROL OVER BODILY EXPRESSIONS'.

About 1.6 million years ago, Homo erectus began dominating the world. They harnessed fire, cooked both meat and tubers and made the first hand-axes, stone tools thought to have been used as symbols to attract the opposite sex. Their readiness to invent and adopt 'culture', improved nutrition and stimulation resulting from the conquering of new lands led to a significant increase in brain size and a growing human-like intelligence. Homo erectus were great voyagers, venturing far out of an original African homeland into both north and south-east Asia. Between 800,000 and 900,000 years ago, Homo erectus' technology allowed them to successfully cross great expanses of sea, even colonising the island of Flores on Australia's doorstep.

THROUGHOUT THIS PERIOD, AND PERHAPS MUCH EARLIER, HUMAN ANCESTORS WERE ATTRACTED TO BRIGHT, COLOURFUL STONE AND OTHER UNUSUAL NATURAL OBJECTS. FOR INSTANCE, THE EARLIEST EVIDENCE OF MINED OCHRE DATES TO 900,000 YEARS AGO. SOME ARCHAEOLOGISTS BELIEVE THAT BRIGHT MATERIALS WERE USED IN SEXUAL AND OTHER DISPLAY, BY BOTH SEXES FROM AN EARLY ERA, AND THAT THESE SUBSTANCES WERE THE SUBJECT OF COMPETITION, NEGOTIATION AND EVEN MONOPOLISATION. IF PIGMENTS WERE USED IN THIS WAY, THEY WERE MOST PORTABLE IF APPLIED TO THE BODY. INDEED, IT IS QUITE PROBABLE THAT BRIGHTLY COLOURED PIGMENTS BEGAN TO BE APPLIED TO THE BODY SOON AFTER HAIR LOSS.

Unfortunately, most body art is made of perishable material, such as flesh and bone, and does not preserve well. But about 200,000 years ago, evidence of body art suddenly becomes more apparent in the archaeological record. Not only was ochre widely used but also perforated pendants were worn. As well, engraved pieces of animal bone have been recovered from many sites with connected double arc and other geometric designs suggestive of body painting, scarification and tattooing.

GIVEN THAT SCARRING FROM NATURAL CAUSES OR INJURY PROBABLY BECAME FREQUENT WITH BODY HAIR LOSS, IT IS QUITE POSSIBLE SCARIFICATION AS BODY ART BEGAN WITH HOMO ERECTUS, UP TO 1.6 MILLION YEARS AGO WHEN MANY OTHER CULTURAL PRACTICES AND INNOVATIONS WERE ADOPTED. TATTOOING WOULD HAVE BEGUN MORE RECENTLY, AS SKIN BECAME LIGHTER IN SOME REGIONS AND AS NEW TOOLS, INKS AND PAINTS WERE DISCOVERED. HOWEVER, THE EARLIEST EVIDENCE IS FROM RELATIVELY RECENT TIMES. IMPORTANTLY, SOME OF THE EARLIEST MUMMIES AND PRESERVED HUMAN BODIES FROM SOUTH AMERICA, EUROPE, AFRICA AND ASIA HAVE TATTOOING AND/OR PURPOSELY MADE SCARS. ÖTZI, THE ICEMAN OF THE EUROPEAN ALPS, FOR INSTANCE, DIED ABOUT 5000 YEARS AGO. WHEN HE WAS FOUND IN 1991 TATTOOS COULD STILL BE SEEN ON HIS LEGS AND ALONG EITHER SIDE OF HIS SPINE. TATTOOING, HOWEVER, IS SOMETHING MORE COMMON TO LIGHT SKINNED PEOPLES; SCARIFICATION IS THE EQUIVALENT FOR THOSE WITH DARKER SKINS. BUT TATTOOS AND SCARS OFTEN SERVE

SIMILAR FUNCTIONS, SIGNALLING AN INDIVIDUAL'S SOCIAL POSITION, STATUS, SEXUAL READINESS OR AVAILABILITY AND DEGREE OF INITIATION OR KNOWLEDGE ATTAINMENT. THEY TELL BOTH FRIENDS AND FOE HOW ONE SHOULD BE TREATED AS WELL AS DEFINING FOR ONESELF HOW TO ACT IN CERTAIN SITUATIONS.

One of the reasons scarification is primarily practiced by dark-skinned people is that their skin contains keloid, a substance that produces a raised scar. Conversely, light skinned people have little keloid but battle, operation or sporting scars, such as European duelling scars, war wounds, scars from animal attacks and so forth, often are proudly displayed by both light and dark skinned individuals as marks of courage or stories of survival. Perhaps the first purposely made scars were meant to mimic or symbolically express similar aspects of bravery and endurance.

IN MANY WAYS, TATTOOING AND SCARIFICATION CAN SOMETIMES BE VIEWED AS OPPOSITES THAT ARE PART OF THE SAME PROCESS OF PERMANENTLY MARKING THE BODY WITH SYMBOLIC DESIGNS. HOWEVER, OCCASIONALLY THEY ARE USED SIMULTANEOUSLY WITHIN THE SAME COMMUNITY. THE MAORI MOKO IS AN INTERESTING CASE AS IT COMBINES FACIAL TATTOOING WITH DEEPLY CUT SCARS TO PRODUCE A TRULY UNIQUE EFFECT. IMPORTANTLY, MOKO ALSO IS APPLIED VERY DIFFERENTLY TO MEN AND WOMEN, MEN'S DESIGNS USUALLY BEING MUCH MORE ELABORATE AND EXTENSIVE, DEPENDING ON STATUS. FURTHERMORE, THERE ARE STATUS AND AGE DIFFERENCES, WITH EACH GEOMETRIC ELEMENT HAVING BOTH PERSONAL AND GROUP MEANING. MORE ANCIENT TATTOO AND SCARIFICATION DESIGNS FROM VARIOUS CORNERS OF THE GLOBE MAY HAVE FUNCTIONED SIMILARLY BUT WE WILL NEVER RECOVER THEIR EXACT MEANING.

In recent times, the main motivations for purposeful scarification are as part of an initiation or ceremony, status symbol, to make more attractive to the opposite sex or, in parts of northern Australia, to protect against/ward off certain harmful spirits. But in some societies, especially those with peoples that have light skins, there is an aversion to scars — they are considered 'ugly', especially if on the face or other body parts thought to be key points of 'beauty'. However, among dark skinned groups, scars on the face, buttocks, back or other body parts may be considered to be especially attractive. Body art expert Julian Robinson (1998:85) has summarised some of the motivations for scarification:

MOST FORMS OF TRIBAL SCARS ARE MADE IN TRADITIONAL DESIGNS OR PATTERNED GROUPS ON SPECIFIC PARTS OF THE BODY AS AN INDIVIDUAL PASSES THROUGH VARIOUS STAGES OF LIFE — WHAT MIGHT BE DESCRIBED AS WRITTEN EVIDENCE OF A PERSON'S "RITES OF PASSAGE" — THUS DENOTING THE PRECISE SOCIAL STATUS OF EACH INDIVIDUAL. THESE PATTERNS ARE ALSO PERCEIVED AS SYMBOLS OF TRIBAL BEAUTY FOR THOSE ABLE TO DECIPHER THE MESSAGES CONVEYED, AND GIVE A UNIQUE SCULPTURED QUALITY TO THE BODY, WHICH IS WIDELY ADMIRED. CICATRIX SCAR PATTERNS ARE ALSO WIDELY USED — THEY ARE A CONTROLLED LONG FLAT SHINY SCAR FORMED BY CAREFULLY CUTTING THE SURFACE OF THE SKIN WITH THE DESIGN REQUIRED, EASING THE WOUND APART SLIGHTLY AND THEN INFLAMING THE OPEN CUT WITH GROUND ASH MIXED WITH A LITTLE FRUIT JUICE OR OTHER IRRITANT SO THAT WHEN HEALED A FLAT SHINY SCAR FORMS.

IN ADDITION TO ITS SYMBOLIC MEANING, SCARRING CAN ALSO PLAY AN IMPORTANT ROLE IN PREVENTIVE MEDICINE NOT REALISED BY MANY WESTERN OBSERVERS: THE BODY BUILDS UP ITS ANTIBODIES DURING THE GRADUAL SCARRING PROCESS, SO THAT THE MATURE ADULT IS MORE ABLE TO SURVIVE IN THE HARSH CONDITIONS OF BUSH LIFE.

A common feature of scarification, and indeed all body art, is that of cultural attitudes and identity. For instance, among certain peoples of the South Pacific and northern Africa, tattooing helps distinguish them from their darker skinned neighbours, as well as reflecting cultural experiences or rites of passage. But many marks on bodies are hidden, reserved for use and display in more private circumstances. For instance, there has long been a concern, fascination or even preoccupation with modifying both male and female genitals. It is not something new to paint, tattoo, scar, pierce or modify a penis, clitoris or labia. Some Egyptian mummies over 6000 years old show evidence of genital modification. Today, some men risk setting off metal detectors at airports with sometimes dozens of pieces of metal through penis and scrotum. Obviously, there is a fine line between pleasure and pain when it comes to self-expression and control. And titillation, machismo and flamboyance all feature when it comes to sex. So it is only natural to expect some of the most richly adorned parts of the body to be the genitals. Many people wear brightly coloured underwear at least on occasion while others feel quite at home in lace, leather or jewel encrusted cod pieces. Think of the bold statement of identity a pair of white Y-fronts makes!

CONCEALMENT — THE OBSCURING OF PHYSICAL FEATURES — IS A KEY FEATURE OF MANY FORMS OF BODY ART, NOT JUST THAT TO DO WITH GENITALS. CONCEALMENT IS OBVIOUS IN CERTAIN FORMS OF CLOTHING, SUCH AS A CATHOLIC NUN'S HABIT, MUSLIM DRESS AND BATHING COSTUMES FROM VICTORIAN ENGLAND. MASKS ARE A STRIKING FORM OF BODY ART THAT BOTH CONCEAL THE FACE AND TRANSFORM PERSONAL IDENTITY. OFTEN THEY ARE COMBINED WITH COSTUME IN ORDER TO PORTRAY THE IDENTITY OF AN ANCESTOR, MYTHOLOGICAL BEING OR HERO. THE NEW IDENTITY IS ACTED OUT IN RITUAL PERFORMANCE, WITH MANY PEOPLE BELIEVING THE BEINGS REPRESENTED ARE ACTUALLY PRESENT. THE ACTORS THEMSELVES TAKE ON THE POWER OF THE BEINGS THEY PORTRAY AND, IN THE PROCESS, CAN REACH A HIGHER STATE OF AWARENESS, BEING, SELF-EXPRESSION AND SELF-CONFIDENCE. MASKS ARE A FORM OF BODY ART WHICH ACT OUT TRANSFORMATION, REPLACING ONE IDENTITY WITH ANOTHER AND EXPRESSING CATEGORICAL CHANGE. THEY OCCUR IN CONNECTION WITH RITES OF PASSAGE AND CURATIVE CEREMONIES SUCH AS EXORCISMS; THEY ARE FREQUENTLY ASSOCIATED WITH FUNERARY RITES AND DEATH. BUT THEY ALSO CAN BE ABOUT LIFE, RENEWED LIFE AND REBIRTH. SOMETIMES, WE APPLY A COSMETIC OR MUD FACE MASK TO RENEW AND REJUVENATE OUR FACE. IN THE PROCESS, WE ATTEMPT TO ACCENTUATE AND BRING OUR FACIAL FEATURES ALIVE TO ATTRACT SEXUAL PARTNERS. OR WE DON A MASK ALONG WITH A NEW PERSONA FOR A FANCY DRESS BALL, A HALLOWEEN DANCE, MARDI GRAS PERFORMANCE OR DURING WAR — TO PLAY, TO ACT AND TO PASS ON TO ANOTHER STATE OF BEING.

Wigs, hair, hats and headdresses are also meant to transform and bring attention to our faces and heads. They signal status, hierarchy, initiation, sexual orientation, competence and competition. Compare the primarily male hats and headdresses worn by members of the Catholic church, from the Pope, to cardinals, bishops and priests to the female *headgear displayed annually at the great Australian festival called the Melbourne Cup. Then think of wigs worn by judges, barristers, lawyers, prostitutes, drag queens and harlots. Hippy hair, Rasta hair, pink hair, Mohawks, lime green, red and blue.*

ENORMOUS AND ELABORATE HEADDRESSES WERE WORN BY AUSTRALIAN ABORIGINAL MALES IN ARNHEM LAND AND THE KIMBERLEY OVER 10,000 YEARS AGO IF ROCK PAINTING DEPICTIONS ARE AN INDICATION. EARLY EXPLORERS AND ANTHROPOLOGISTS WITH STEREOTYPICAL PITH HELMETS WOULD HAVE LOVED TO HAVE ENCOUNTERED THEM IN THE FLESH. BOWLER HATS, AUSSIE AKUBRAS, BASEBALL CAPS WORN BACKWARDS, SOMBREROS, YARMULKES, SUNDAY HATS, SCARVES, CARMEN MIRANDA'S HEAD OF FRUIT, WIDOW'S CAPS, CROWNS, TIARAS, MILITARY HATS AND HELMETS, BRIDAL VEILS, TOWERING PACIFIC ISLAND HEADDRESSES AND INDIAN TURBANS ARE JUST A FEW OF THE MANY FORMS OF HEAD ADORNMENT EXPRESSING CULTURAL AFFILIATION, STATUS, RELIGIOUS BELIEF, STATE OF BEING AND PERSONAL IDENTITY. THEY DRAW ATTENTION DIRECTLY TO OR ABOVE THE FACE, FORCING THE VIEWER TO MAKE CONTACT AND SIGNAL THE NATURE OF INTERACTION THAT SHOULD TAKE PLACE.

A concern for personal identity and portraying such through body art begins at an early age. As infants begin to explore their new world with hands and eyes, they soon learn to recognise parents, siblings and friends. They learn the identities of other people partly through the ways these people adorn themselves and are taught to follow similar practices. If they are girls in southern Europe, they might have their ears pierced at a very early age; if they are boys in Israel or the USA, they might have their penises circumcised. They are dressed, painted and otherwise adorned. In some parts of the world, they might receive their first tattoo before the age of one. Today, in many countries, their faces are painted for ceremony, fun and profit. Eventually, they might acquire lip plugs, neck bands, ear spools, nose rings, anklets, navel jewellery or bones through the nose.

SOME CHILDREN QUICKLY EXPRESS STREAKS OF INDEPENDENCE, WANTING TO CHOOSE CLOTHES OR CHANGE THE APPEARANCE OF THEIR HAIR BEFORE THE AGE OF TWO. OTHERS PATIENTLY SIT BACK, WATCHING AND LEARNING THE NORMS OF THEIR FAMILY, SOCIETY AND CULTURAL GROUP UNTIL ONE DAY THEY WILL IMITATE THEM. BUT WHICHEVER THE CASE, CHILDREN QUICKLY LEARN THE 'PROPER' CODES OF DRESS AND ADORNMENT. WHETHER THEY CONSISTENTLY FOLLOW THESE RULES IS ANOTHER MATTER, WITH TEENAGERS EVERYWHERE OFTEN REBELLING OR PROTESTING ADULT WAYS BY PURPOSELY ADORNING THEMSELVES AGAINST COMMON PRACTICE. IN WESTERN SOCIETY THIS HAS BECOME SO PREVALENT THAT WHOLE SUBCULTURES HAVE ARISEN WITH THEIR OWN RULES AND MODES OF BODY ART AND PRACTICE. THE CONSEQUENCE IS THAT TODAY, IN MODERN DAY AUSTRALIA, AMERICA OR EUROPE, TO GET A TATTOO OR PIERCING MIGHT MORE BE AN EXPRESSION OF CONFORMING RATHER THAN REBELLING. INTERESTINGLY, IN RECENT YEARS THERE HAS BEEN A MOVEMENT TOWARD INDIGENOUS TATTOO DESIGNS AMONG WESTERN YOUTH AND A COMPARABLE INVERSE PREFERENCE TOWARD WESTERN DESIGNS BY THE YOUNG OF THE PACIFIC ISLANDS AND OTHER TRADITIONAL TATTOO-PRACTISING NATIONS. AND EVEN SOME BIKIE GANGS ARE CHANGING FROM HEAVY METAL AND ROSE DESIGNS TO ELABORATE DISPLAYS OF NATIVE AUSTRALIAN FLOWERS, SOMETIMES REVEALING GLIMPSES OF THE OPERA HOUSE OR EVEN THE SYDNEY HARBOUR BRIDGE.

Body shaping is another area that has undergone a transformation in recent times. Head binding, neck stretching, foot binding and corsets were once all the rage in some cultures. Tooth filing, finger amputation, lip stretching and ear elongation were also practiced in a variety of ceremonial and cultural contexts. Then came face lifts, nose jobs, tooth rearrangement by specialists called 'orthodontists' and breast implants. Today, changes to the shape of one's body are limited only by money and imagination. Liposuction, the vacuuming of fat from under the skin, is increasingly being used to lose weight quickly — to shape and sculpt into a 'new you'. Nips and tucks can be performed almost anywhere one desires, the length or width of the penis can be increased and almost any blemish considered unsightly can be removed. Plastic surgery is not just for accident victims but more often is a tool for body art. However, this form of body art can be particularly painful, expensive and time-consuming, a sacrifice that many feel is worth making because of the resulting perceived attractiveness, self-confidence and self-esteem.

FOR MANY PEOPLE, THE MORE TIME, DEDICATION, PAIN AND TOIL PUT INTO THEIR ADORNMENT, THE MORE THEY FEEL EMPOWERED. IN GROUP SETTINGS, THIS IS OFTEN ASSOCIATED WITH SOME FORM OF INITIATION, AND INITIATION ALWAYS INVOLVES SACRIFICE AND CONFRONTATION. FOR INDIVIDUALS, THE PAIN AND ENDURANCE OF SOME FORMS OF BODY ART MIMIC THOSE OF GROUP INITIATION, GIVING HIGHS WORTH REPEATING. FOR OTHERS, THEIR BODY IS A LIFE'S WORK, A PIECE OF PERFORMANCE ART THAT IS CONTINUALLY BEING REFINED AND ADDED TO. IN EXTREMES, THIS LEADS TO EVERY PART OF THE BODY BEING TATTOOED, FROM HEAD TO FOOT. OR IT MAY LEAD TO AN ECLECTIC COMPOSITION OF INK, STEEL, SCAR TISSUE, ANIMAL PRODUCTS, CLOTHING AND PRECIOUS STONES SET ON A SCULPTED HUMAN FORM THAT CONTINUALLY CHANGES WITH THE APPLICATION OF PAINTS, DYES AND HAIR-PIECES. FOR MANY PEOPLE, THEIR BODY IS THEIR ART, AS WELL AS AN EXPRESSION OF A HISTORY OF PERSONAL AND GROUP EXPERIENCE.

And everyone practises some form of body art. We might have rings or other forms of jewellery that symbolise graduation, engagement, marriage, a birthday or a personal milestone. We cut and shape our hair in ways that reflect both personal and cultural tastes, styles and practices. Some of us grow facial hair into elaborate, intricate or outrageously ragged patterns. We cloth ourselves in all manner of material, substance and colour. We mark our skin with temporary or long-lasting designs — scarred, burnt, tattooed, dusted and painted on both very intimate and very publicly accessible parts of the body. We have elaborate traditions that celebrate status, rites of passage, religious beliefs and cultural histories. Some of us change our shapes through a variety of time consuming and, often, painful practices. Some of us eat to look fat; others diet to look thin. We may hold different ideas of what constitutes 'beauty' but we share an ideal that 'beauty' exists, both for ourselves and for others. This is one of the things being human is all about.

BUT WHAT OF THE FUTURE? WHAT NEW, BOLD, SHOCKING AND STUNNINGLY BEAUTIFUL BODY ART CAN WE EXPECT OVER THE NEXT MILLENNIUM? PERHAPS BODY MODIFICATION WILL BE TAKEN TO NEW HEIGHTS WITH INTERCHANGEABLE FACES, COMPLETE SCALP AND HAIR TRANSPLANTS, WRINKLE-PROOF HANDS AND EVEN THE ADDITION OF ANIMAL BODY PARTS BECOMING COMMON. CERTAINLY, NEW FORMS OF MARKING AND MODIFYING THE SKIN WILL BE INVENTED, SUCH AS PERMANENT CHANGES TO SKIN COLOUR, IMPLANTS THAT PROJECT OUTWARD INTO A MYRIAD OF FASHIONABLE FORMS AND NEW TYPES OF TATTOOING, SUCH AS 3D DESIGNS OR CHANGING/SHIFTING PATTERNS TRIGGERED BY VARIABLE LIGHTING. PERHAPS EVEN THE CYBORG MACHINE-BODY FUSIONS OF SCIENCE FICTION FILMS WILL SOON BE POSSIBLE. ONE DAY WE MAY BE ABLE TO GENETICALLY ENGINEER INTERCHANGEABLE BODY PARTS, CHANGING SHAPES, HEIGHTS, COLOURS AND TEXTURES FOR DIFFERENT OCCASIONS. ONLY TIME AND HUMAN IMAGINATION WILL TELL BUT IT IS PREDICTED VARIATION WILL INCREASE RATHER THAN DECREASE AS PEOPLE SEARCH FOR NEW WAYS TO EXPRESS THEMSELVES IN AN EVER CHANGING, TECHNOLOGICALLY-DRIVEN WORLD. OUR BODIES WILL REMAIN DEEPLY PERSONAL. PERHAPS THEY WILL ALSO REMAIN THE ONE ASPECT OF OUR LIVES OVER WHICH WE WILL HAVE SOME MEASURE OF CONTROL.

Dr. Paul S.C. Taçon
Head of the People and Place Research Centre
Australian Museum
February 2000

FURTHER READING

KING, M. 1992. MOKO: MAORI TATTOOING IN THE 20TH CENTURY. DAVID BATEMAN, AUCKLAND.

Robinson, J. 1998. The quest for human beauty: an illustrated history. W.W. Norton & Co., New York.

RUBIN, A. (ED.). 1988. MARKS OF CIVILISATION: ARTISTIC TRANSFORMATIONS OF THE HUMAN BODY. UNIVERSITY OF CALIFORNIA, LOS ANGELES.

Sherratt, A. 1999. The Thak hypothesis: a prestige-good model of early hominine behaviour. Cambridge Archaeological Journal. 9(2):277-85.

TAÇON, P.S.C. 1999. ALL THINGS BRIGHT AND BEAUTIFUL: THE ROLE AND MEANING OF COLOUR IN HUMAN DEVELOPMENT. CAMBRIDGE ARCHAEOLOGICAL JOURNAL. 9(1):120-26.

Taylor, T. 1997. The prehistory of sex: four million years of human sexual culture. Fourth Estate, London.

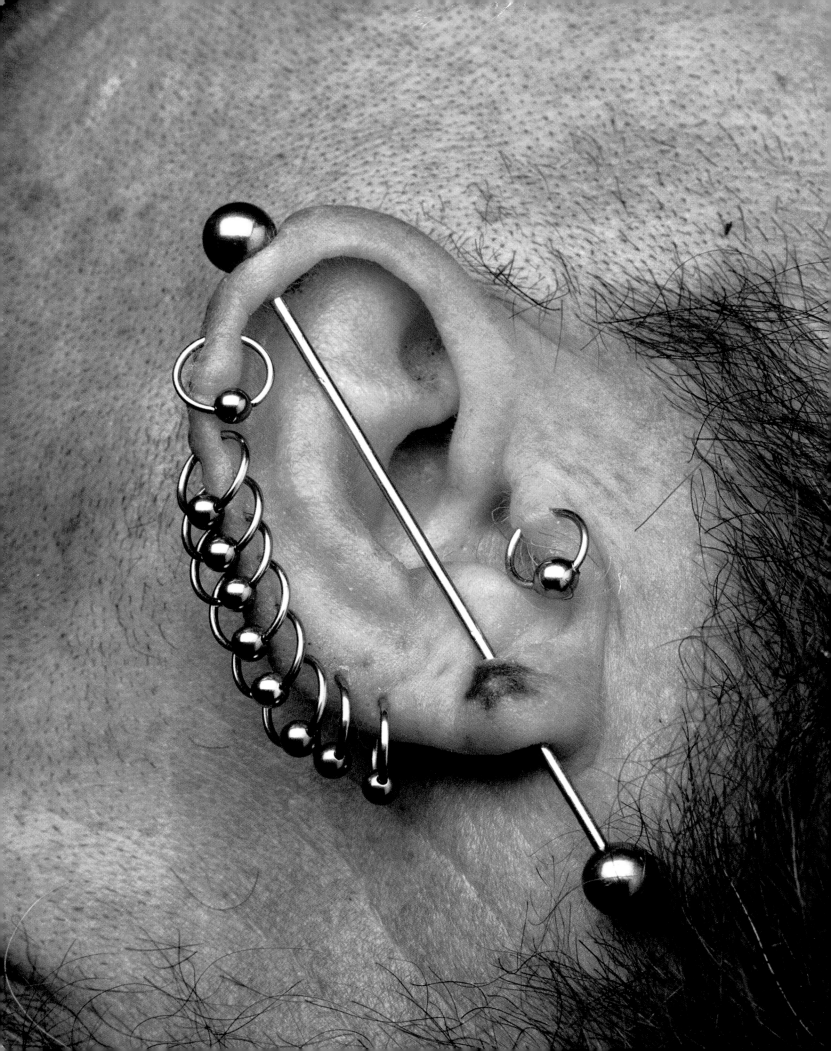

Pierce-Paul

mple,
ep

my body.

If my body was a temple, you'd decorate the walls... that's why I decorate my body.

Piercer Paul

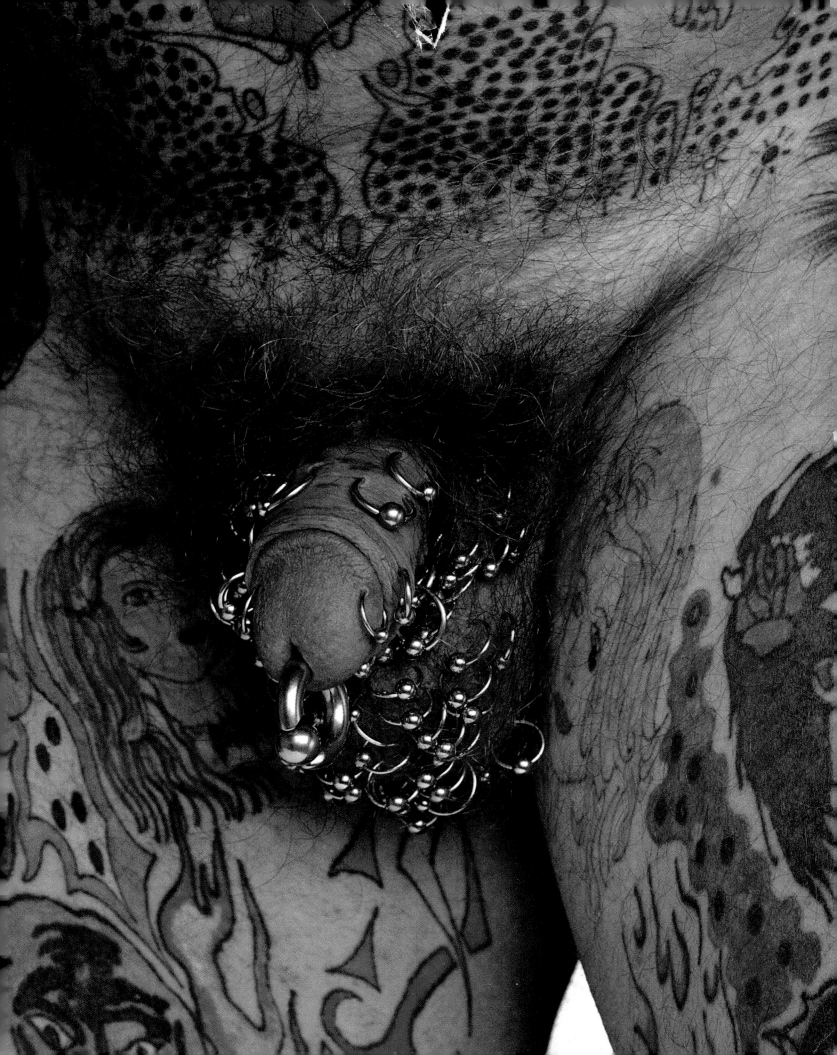

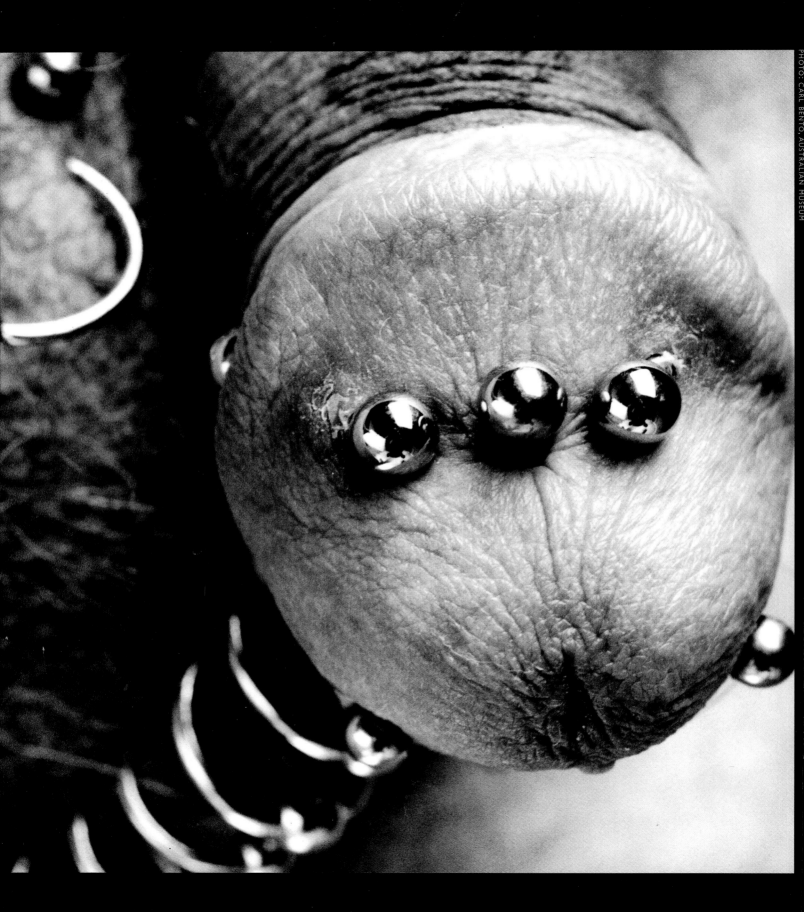

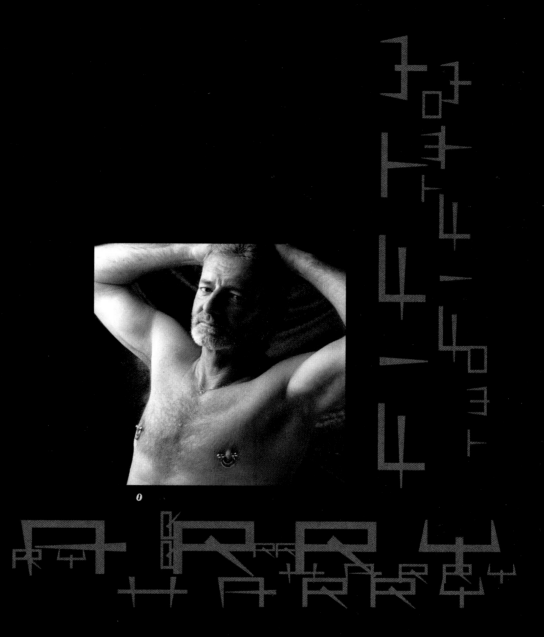

FIFTY

FIFTY

THREE

FOUR

HARRY

HARRY

" I'VE ONLY GOT ONE REGRET...

REGRET... THAT I

THAT I DIDN'T DO IT SOONER."

HARRY, 52

the piercing process

A female genital piercing being done.

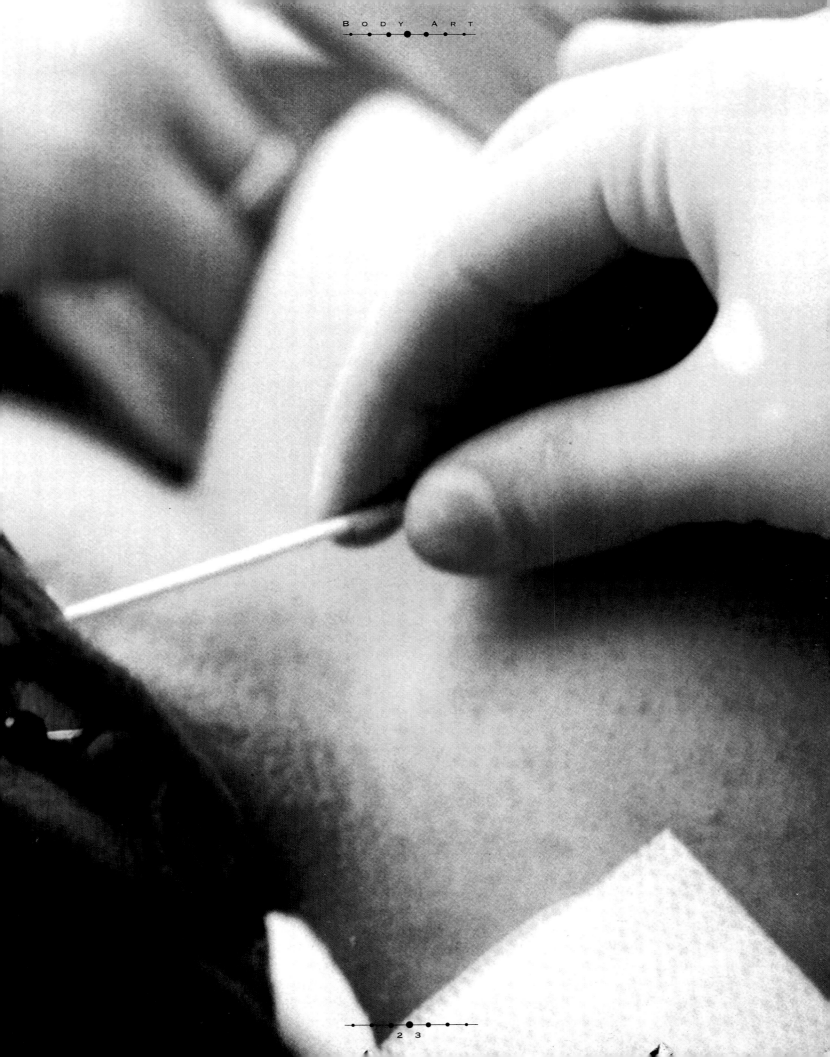

MISTRESS

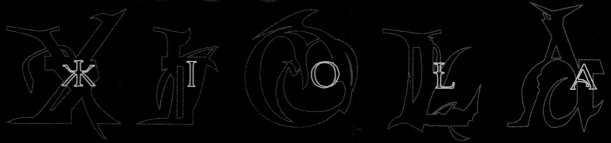

XIOLA

PIERCING = PAIN = PLEASURE

Piercing Equals Pain Equals Pleasure Modification Equals Pain Equals Pleasure
Piercing Equals Pain Equals Pleasure Modification Equals Pain Equals Pleasure
Piercing Equals Pain Equals Pleasure Modification Equals Pain Equals Pleasure
Piercing Equals Pain Equals Pleasure Modification Equals Pain Equals Pleasure
piercing equals pain equals pleasure modification equals pain equals pleasure
Piercing Equals Pain Equals Pleasure Modification Equals Pain Equals Pleasure
Piercing Equals Pain Equals Pleasure Modification Equals Pain Equals Pleasure
Piercing Equals Pain Equals Pleasure Modification Equals Pain Equals Pleasure
Piercing Equals Pain Equals Pleasure Modification Equals Pain Equals Pleasure
Piercing Equals Pain Equals Pleasure Modification Equals Pain Equals Pleasure
piercing equals pain equals pleasure modification equals pain equals pleasure
Piercing Equals Pain Equals Pleasure Modification Equals Pain Equals Pleasure
Piercing Equals Pain Equals Pleasure Modification Equals Pain Equals Pleasure
Piercing Equals Pain Equals Pleasure Modification Equals Pain Equals Pleasure
Piercing Equals Pain Equals Pleasure Modification Equals Pain Equals Pleasure
Piercing Equals Pain Equals Pleasure Modification Equals Pain Equals Pleasure
piercing equals pain equals pleasure modification equals pain equals pleasure
Piercing Equals Pain Equals Pleasure Modification Equals Pain Equals Pleasure
Piercing Equals Pain Equals Pleasure Modification Equals Pain Equals Pleasure
Piercing Equals Pain Equals Pleasure Modification Equals Pain Equals Pleasure
Piercing Equals Pain Equals Pleasure Modification Equals Pain Equals Pleasure

MODIFICATION = PAIN = PLEASURE

Mistress
Xiola, DOMINATRIX, 26

BRETT

Temporary piercing: there's a certain taboo about it whi
territory and an element of fear and pain – all these
breaking taboos, going that extra step. It also involve
and giving all control to them, but being able to choo

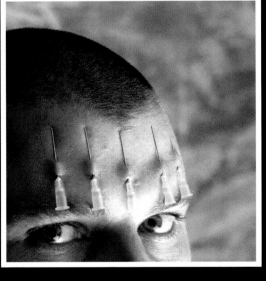

Permanent piercing: Even though it's my
a permanent reminder of him. I like to
sort of person I am because of my pierc
Sean Bates

Piercing is a very personal, very rituali
to be shared with my lover. It provides
Brett Quinlan

 E A Π

...as a certain attraction. the thrill of going into dangerous
...s in combination provide an adrenalin rush. It's about
...ting down your guard, giving yourself as a blank canvas
...ho to give the control to.

...ce to get it done, it's like a gift from Brett and

...k those preconceived notions of what

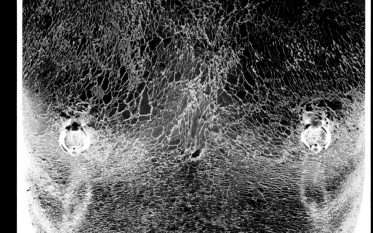

...xperience and something

...d between us.

...TES, DIRECTOR, FUSE ADVERTISING, 30

RETT QUINLAN, CLOTHES DESIGNER, 25

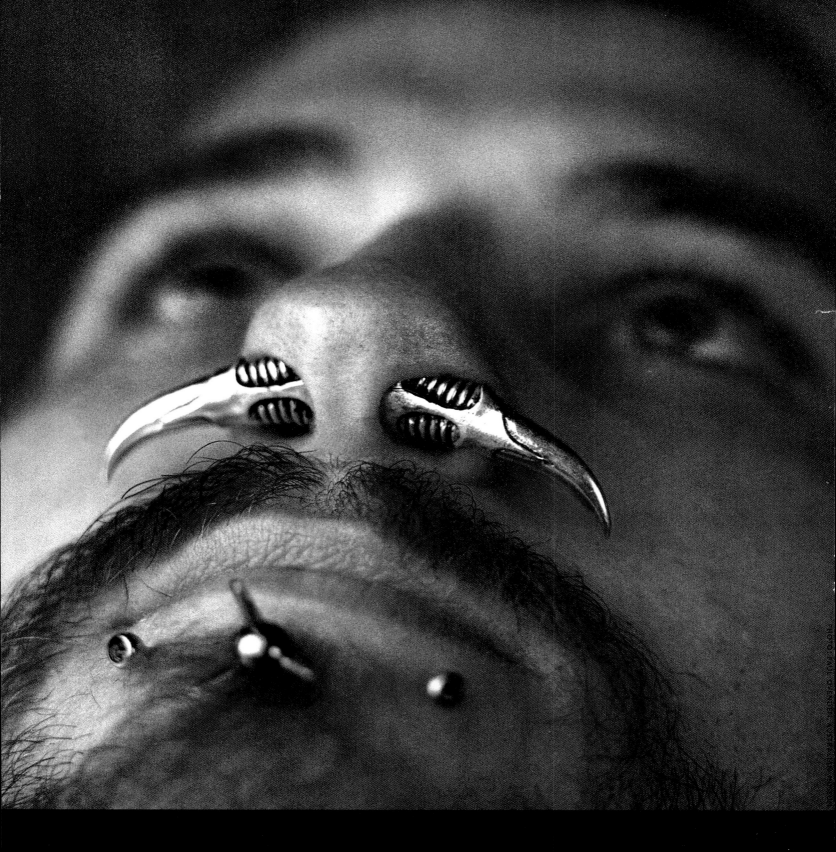

DARREN

It's about a rediscovery of my identity and my deep connection with nature.
I am in control, I am myself 'no labels' it's not fashion, it's about feeling alive!

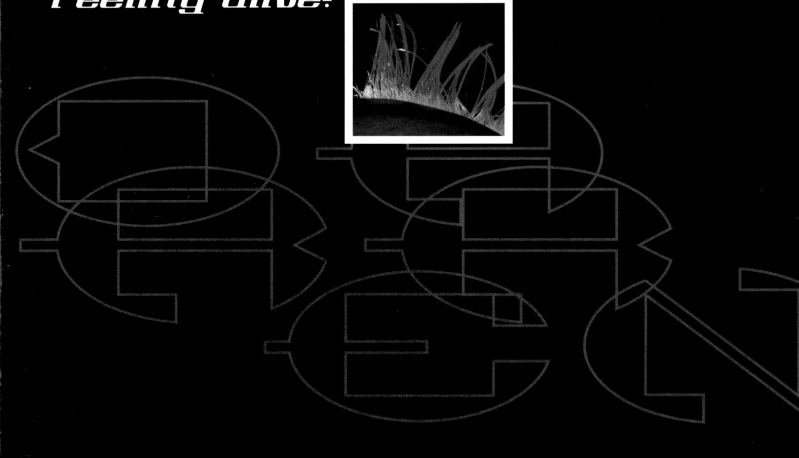

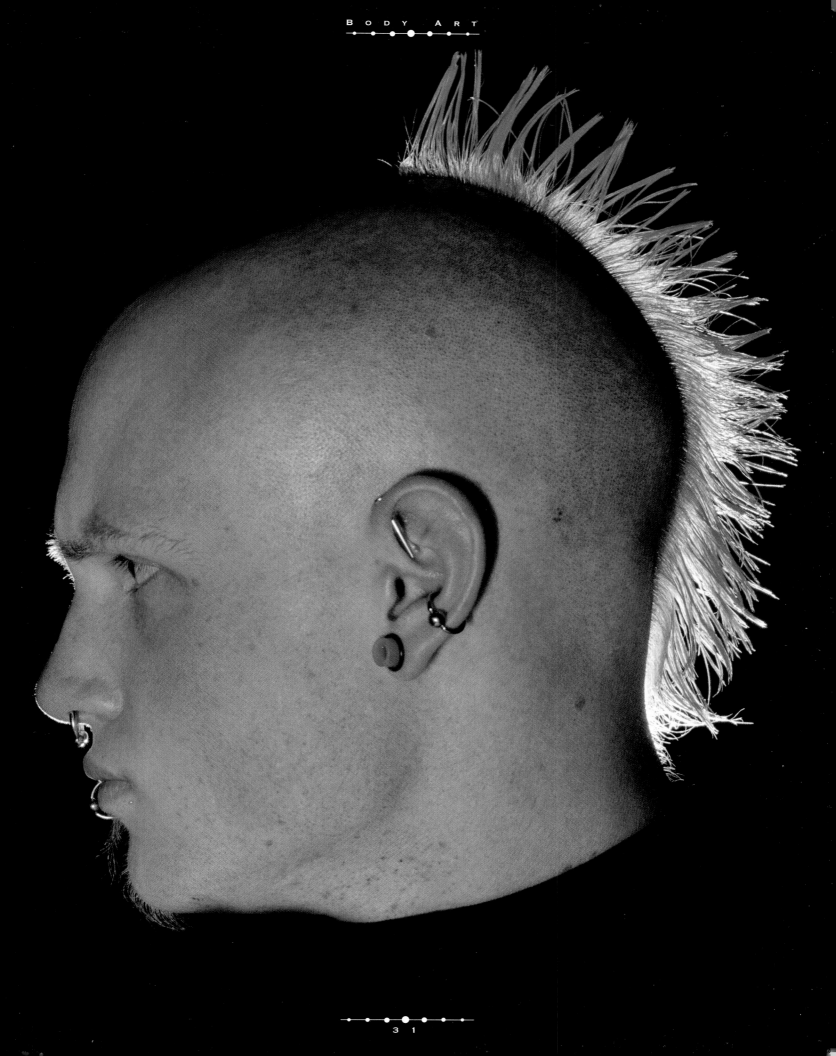

Life can be so drab and dreary and numbing. Piercing makes me aware I am alive. Some people pinch themselves to make sure they're not dreaming. I prefer the marriage of metal and flesh. My body had been owned by so many other people but when I made the decision to feel pain, I felt powerful once again. My body wasn't mine until I claimed it through piercing.

Kate, 18

For the most part of my life, I've felt like an outsider looking in. Even at the best of times. I've always felt alien in social situations...different in kind by nature and composition. The way in which I physically represent myself is an embodiment of the disassociation I feel with the majority of people. My piercings are a prominent and permanent reminder of this awareness. They make me feel less human and more human at the same time. They mean much more than just a vain form of conceit or embellishment. It was a personal visualisation and affirmation of the slow process of metamorphosis I was and am still currently going through. A transition into a radiant swan, from the ugly duckling I've always felt that I have been.

Joanne,
Shop Assistant, 18

*R*eed

ARTS ADMINISTRATOR, 2 9

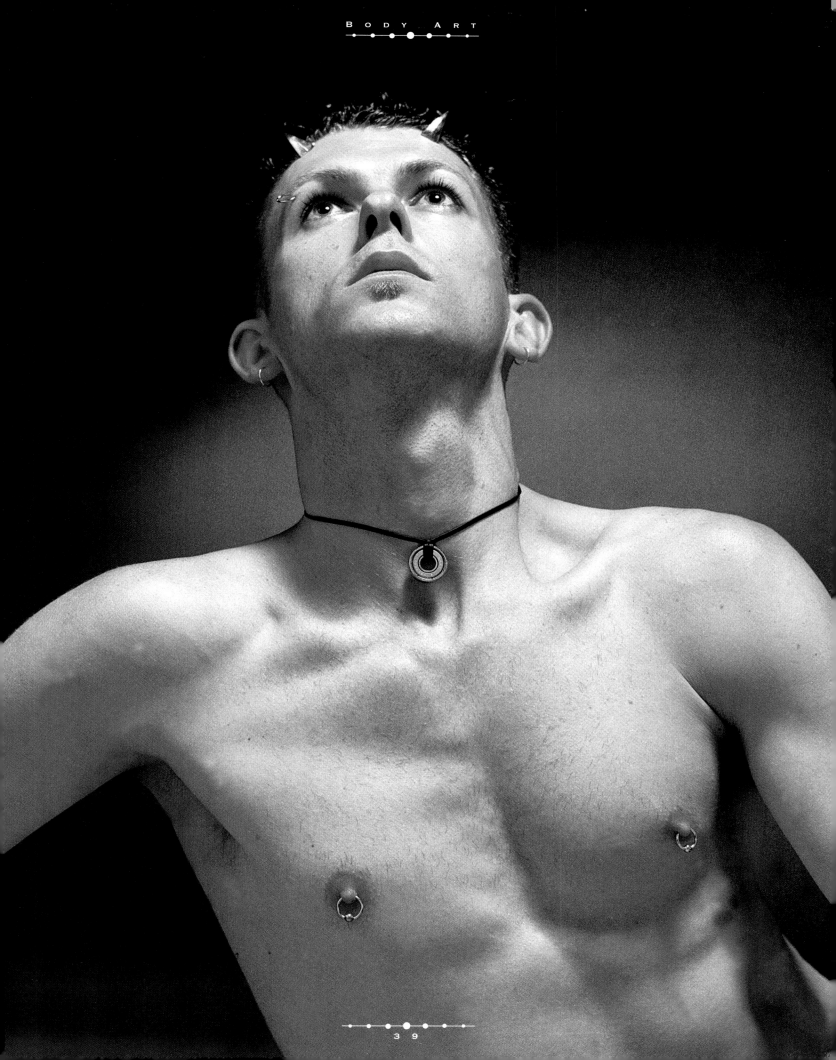

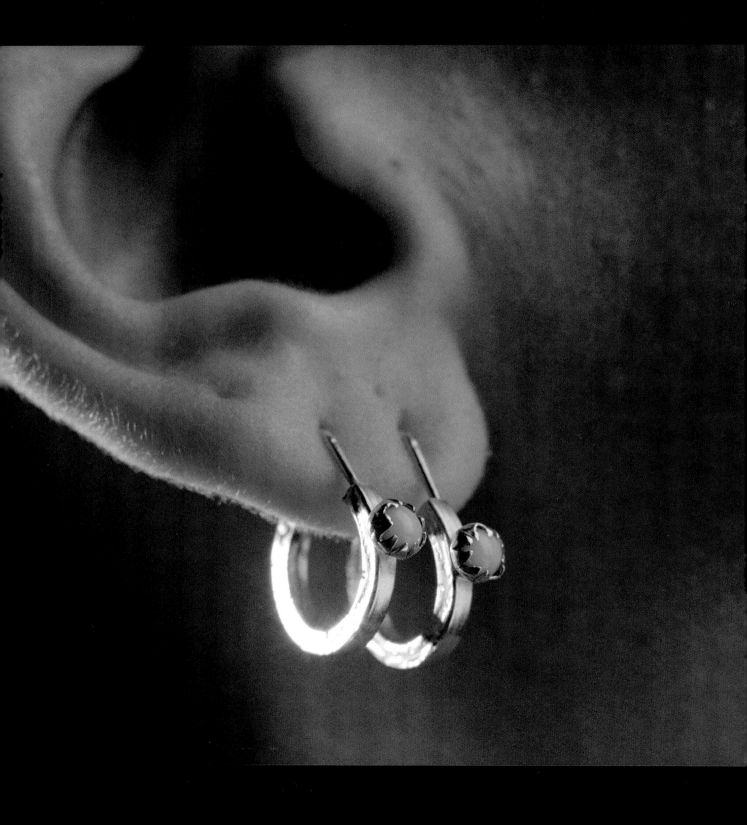

Turquoise and gold are very popular materials in Arabic jewellery. The turquoise is commonly used to ward off the curse of the evil eye . Many babies, when they are born, have a turquoise bead attached to their garments in order to keep them safe from harm. When I turned 12 years

old, my father bought me these earrings from the jewellery bazaar in Tripoli, Lebanon. I kept them in a drawer for a very long time. When I began to wear them, for me it was very symbolic as it represented another way of reclaiming my Arab identity that the 'dominant culture' had forced me to closet for so long.

LISA FADDOUL, ARTS WORKER, 29

Piercings and tattoos are the markings of a

particular period in our life. Time passes and we

wanted to express, remember and symbolise

Sally.Systems Administrator, 23 ~ Bronwyn Griffiths, Student, 19 ~
Elie Köksal, Student, 20 ~ Catherine Aliaga, Student, 18

thoughts, events or phases. It does not represent a

specific type of person or subculture, but our

individual expression.

got my belly button pierced to be rebellious,

but it didn't work. Being pierced on your

belly, for me, felt like being pricked like a

balloon. I continually forget about it and

I'm always surprised to find this little thing

hanging off my belly.

Stella, 15

These performances explore the spirituality of pain where the body is the medium in a ritualised setting. It's about transcendence, releasing pain, embracing fears, releasing fears, embracing pain, balancing control and surrender to focus on the energy spiralling out from a still inner place.

These performances explore the spirituality of pain where the body is the medium in a ritualised setting. It's about transcendence, releasing pain, embracing fears, releasing fears, embracing pain, balancing control and surrender to focus on the energy spiralling out from a still inner place.

AñA Wojak, *Artist*

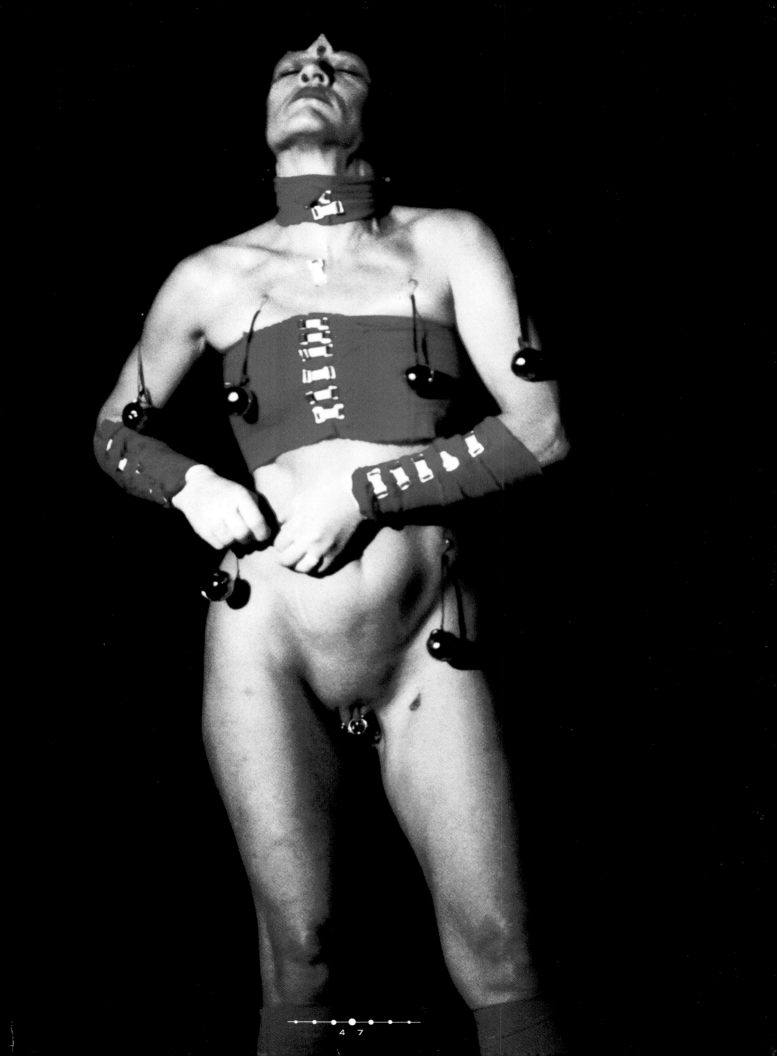

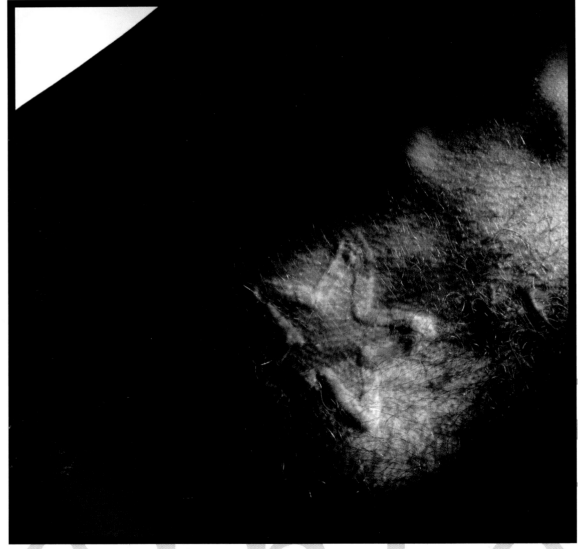

PHOTO: CARL BENTO, AUSTRALIAN MUSEUM

ANDREW GEYL

Body modification can be viewed as a topo-graphical map of a person's emotional and spiritual history. Your whole body can be used to prevent yourself from ever forgetting your mistakes and victories. Each time you look in a mirror, you give yourself the posi-tive reinforcement you have designed for yourself.

BRAND POWER – *feel the heat.*

OTTO

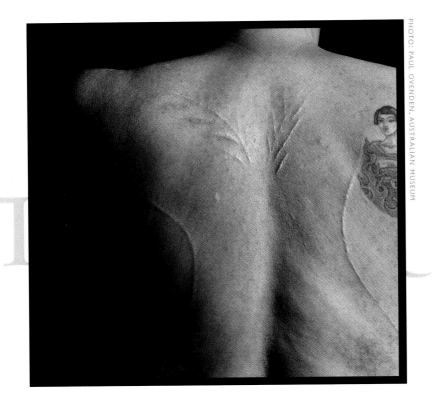

PHOTO: PAUL OVENDEN, AUSTRALIAN MUSEUM

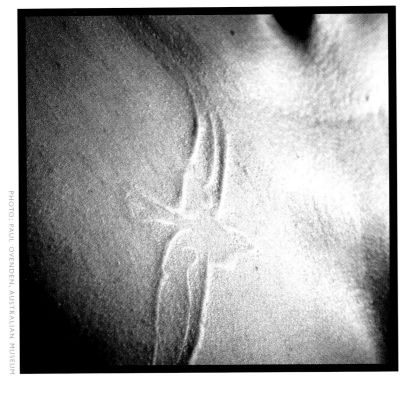

PHOTO: PAUL OVENDEN, AUSTRALIAN MUSEUM

PAULINE

My body adornments are about my inner spirit, love, trust, truth, strength and beauty, which in turn makes up my outward spirit, enabling me to be the strong, brave, loving woman I am.

MY DRAGON DESIGN IS A COMMON TRADITIONAL MOTIF USED IN JAPANESE ART. IT SYMBOLISES WISDOM. MY SURNAME 'TAKIHIRO' IN JAPANESE CHARACTERS AND THE DRAGON DESIGNS HAVE AN UNUSUAL SYNERGY

My dragon design is a common traditional motif

IN MEANING AS THEY BOTH HAVE THE CHARACTERS FOR 'DRAGON' AND 'OCEAN'.

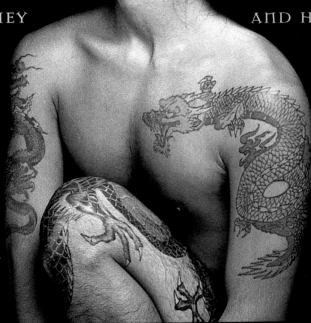

I ALSO HAD A DREAM WHERE I ENCOUNTERED A DRAGON AND THE OCEAN AND I WAS THE 'WHITE HAIRED MAN'. I MET A TOAIST MONK

used in Japanese art. It symbolises wisdom.

AND HE ALSO TOLD ME THERE IS SYNCHRONICITY IN MY DRAGON DESIGN AND MY NAME. WHEN I GOT MY FIRST TATOO IT FELT AS IF MY BODY WAS BURNING. MY FATHER ALSO HAS A TATOO. HE HAS A CHERRY BLOSSOM DESIGN ON HIS BACK.

Ami Takihiro, Musician, 27

I wanted a tattoo ever since
I saw my grandfather's when
I was little. So the tattoo
that means most to me is
the star I have on my wrist,
as it resembles one my
grandfather had.
It gives me a sense of
familial tradition.

CHRISTIAN,
MARTIAL ARTIST, 28

I wanted to do something against people's expectations and break stereotypes.

Why shouldn't aesthetics also be important to a blind person?

It was empowering deciding

to do something to my body

and knowing full well it will be there forever. It was also an ultimate

exercise in trust — putting faith in my friends to help choose the tatoo for me.

Darren Fitler, 25

PHOTO: PAUL OVENDEN, AUSTRALIAN MUSEUM

THE TATTOOLOGIST
SAYS THAT THE
TATTOOEE SHOULD BE
PENETRATED...WE'RE
BLOODY GOOD MATES.

ARM, TATTOOLOGIST AND JEFF RHODES, TATTOO ARTIST

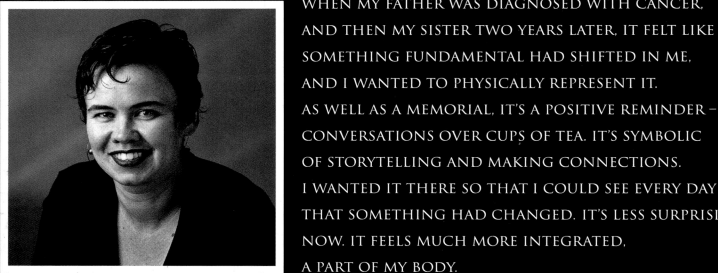

WHEN MY FATHER WAS DIAGNOSED WITH CANCER,
AND THEN MY SISTER TWO YEARS LATER, IT FELT LIKE
SOMETHING FUNDAMENTAL HAD SHIFTED IN ME,
AND I WANTED TO PHYSICALLY REPRESENT IT.
AS WELL AS A MEMORIAL, IT'S A POSITIVE REMINDER –
CONVERSATIONS OVER CUPS OF TEA. IT'S SYMBOLIC
OF STORYTELLING AND MAKING CONNECTIONS.
I WANTED IT THERE SO THAT I COULD SEE EVERY DAY
THAT SOMETHING HAD CHANGED. IT'S LESS SURPRISING
NOW. IT FEELS MUCH MORE INTEGRATED,
A PART OF MY BODY.

The Coptic Orthodox Christians are known to get a tattoo of the Coptic cross on their right hand wrist (in the place where Jesus Christ was nailed) to symbolise their religion. I am proud of my cross. It was through the cross that our lord Jesus Christ gave me salvation. Therefore, in having the cross tattooed on my wrist, I am reminded of Christ's suffering and pain for my sake. It is also a permanent symbol that resembles the permanent salvation I have gained.

Aghabi,

Student, 21

I GOT THESE TATTOOS BECAUSE I WANTED
TO EXPERIENCE THE PAIN, TO SEE IF I
COULD TAKE IT BEFORE GOING AHEAD
WITH A FULL TRADITIONAL MALU
[SAMOAN TATTOO]. ARM AND WRIST
BANDS WERE VERY FASHIONABLE AT THE
TIME. THEY REPRESENT THE TI LEAVES
WHICH THE TAUPOU (CHIEF'S DAUGHTER)
TIES AROUND HER WRISTS AND ARMS
BEFORE DOING THE TRADITIONAL DANCE.

PALOLO NIO, TYPESETTER AND INTERPRETER, 33

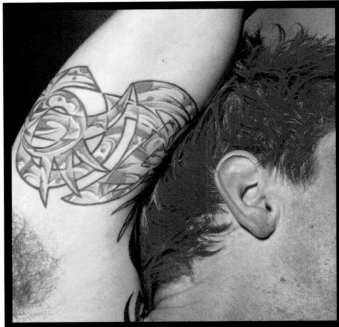

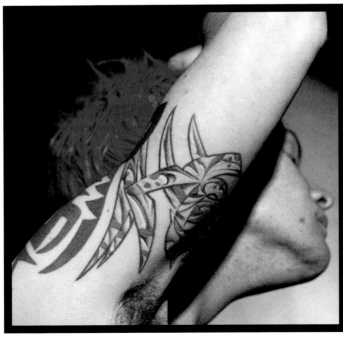

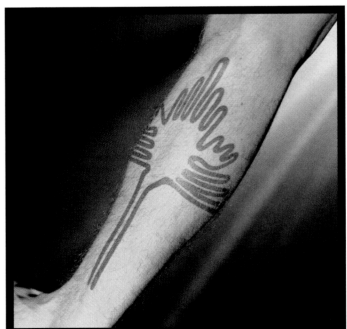

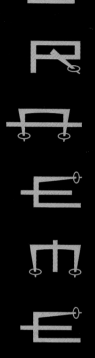

With my tattoos I tend to go for designs which are powerful from a distance. My arm tattoo is an incorporation of both ancient and modern designs, the bold black of traditional styles and the modern urban tribalism of large scale graffiti. The tattoo on my leg is based on the humming-bird of the Nazca Plains in South America, which is visible only from the air. It signifies speed and flight.

Graeme,
Musician, 29

TATTOOING: *a second skin, a manipulation and distortion of the human body, a phenomenon that transgresses boundaries of assumed naturalness, beauty and the immoderate ordering of normative life. I challenge my own fears and desires.*

Sharni, Curator, 25

PHOTO: CARL BENTO, AUSTRALIAN MUSEUM

Elvis, Tutor, 30

My artwork is at once pure aesthetic and aggressively political. It fuses a love of the spectacle of tattooing and constructs me within a process of meaning production that is kinetic and continual. The challenge to subvert dominant discourses concerning body modifications and Western femininity makes the quest impassioned. It is power. it is beauty. it is self.

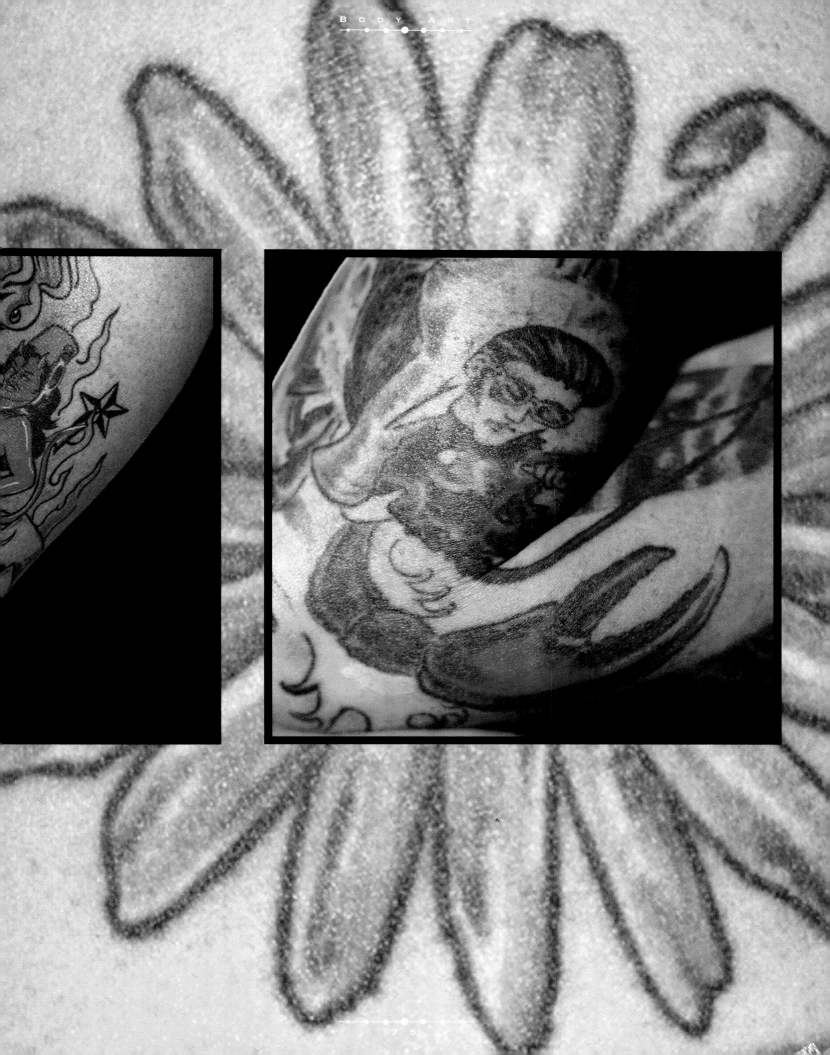

MY TATTOOS NOT ONLY
REPRESENT AND RECOGNISE
ARTISTS I ADMIRE, THEY
ARE A VISUAL INTERPRETATION
OF PERSONAL PAIN/S AND
THE JOURNEY OF MY PSYCHE.
NO REGRETS (ONLY ANTICIPATION).

YOS B WORTH 'HULA DELUX'

PHOTOS: CARL BENTO, AUSTRALIAN MUSEUM

  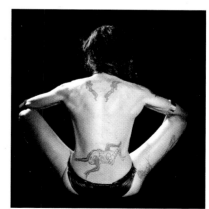

PHOTO: PAUL OVENDEN, AUSTRALIAN MUSEUM

ɪ had a feeling of liberation when ɪ realised that ɪ could do what ɪ liked to my body after the first tattoo and to have the choice to put what ɪ wanted on my body.

I am a freak of wagner's music and my tattoos are inspired by the music of 'ᴛʜe ʀɪng cycle' and its symbolism.

I had always admired seeing tattoos on older guys when ɪ was a young boy but ɪ was too nervous to get one until just in the last few years. As a young boy, ɪ thought that guys that had them looked 'tough', but now, as an adult, ɪ know that it is a myth.

stewart south,
ʀetired, 49

My tattoos tell a story — the story of my life so far — memories of lovers and friends, sadness, growth and knowledge, remembering change and looking to the future, the sacred mark on my skin to wear with pride of who I am. My victory. My rite of passage.

GYPSY, *Artist, 40*

EACH TATTOO
REPRESENTS A DIFFERENT
PART OF MY LIFE — THEY'RE A
STORY ABOUT ME. THEY PORTRAY
ME AND ALL MY PARTS. I HAVE A
MIXTURE OF BLOOD IN ME AND WANTED
THAT REPRESENTED ON MY BODY. THEY
HAVE MERGED WITH ME NOW – THEY ARE
PART OF ME. MY FOREARM TATTOO IS
MADE UP OF TRIANGLES WHICH TO ME
DEPICTS LIFE. LIFE IS NOT SMOOTH,
LIKE THE SPIRAL — LIFE HAS EDGES
AND CORNERS.

NICOLE RANGI DUKE, *Café Barista*, 31

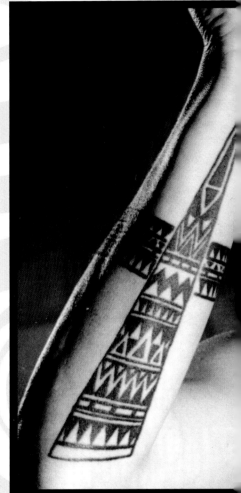

PHOTOS: PAUL OVENDEN, AUSTRALIAN MUSEUM

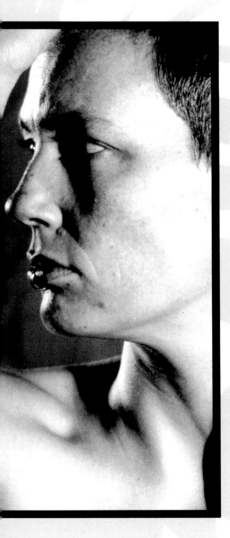

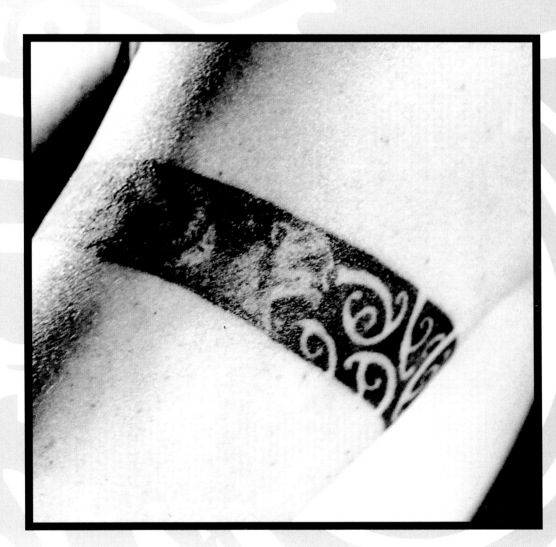

I started getting
tattoos when I was 18 as a
response to my grandfather's death
from Alzheimer's disease. My greatest
fear at that time was that I would die not
being able to remember anything and so
tattooing was a way of making sure I would
remember events of significance. My sleeve design
is based on a story I wrote for my children called
'Yo and Koto' which is about a little fish and a
dragon. I wrote the story after what happened
to Jandamarra O'Shane because I felt that
children should have a big dragon to
protect them.

GLENN GAULD, *Nurse*, 29

PHOTO: CARL BENTO, AUSTRALIAN MUSEUM

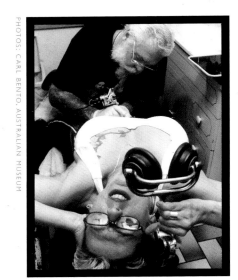

PHOTOS: CARL BENTO, AUSTRALIAN MUSEUM

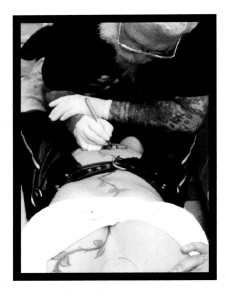

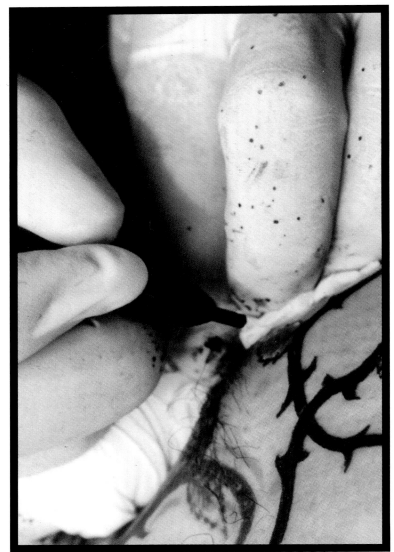

CHANGE CAN BRING ELEMENTS OF DISCOMFORT AND
TURMOIL. IN CONTINUALLY TRYING TO MAINTAIN A
STATIC STATE WE AVOID CHANGE AND GROWTH.

TRIDZIA L. TZAR, *'Tattooed Thorax-An Illustrated Journey'*
(WITH PHOTOS BY ELAINE KITCHENER)

AS I BECOME SPIRITUALLY AWARE, SO DOCUMENTATION
OCCURS IN THE WRITTEN GENRE, IN THE FORM OF
REFLECTIONS... AND A THORNY STEMMED TATTOO
INSCRIBED ON MY BODY.

TRIDZIA

Each of my tattoos is based on a belief system as well as one of the elements. It's about cycles. Everything starts with water. Fire is life — the birth, pain, torment and passion of life. Air is transcending all that, the quieter and later times in life. Earth is the resting stage and from there, all is returned to water. I can always remember who I was with and what I was doing at the time I got the tattoo. They are little sparks for memory.

Ruth Corris, Library Assistant, 23

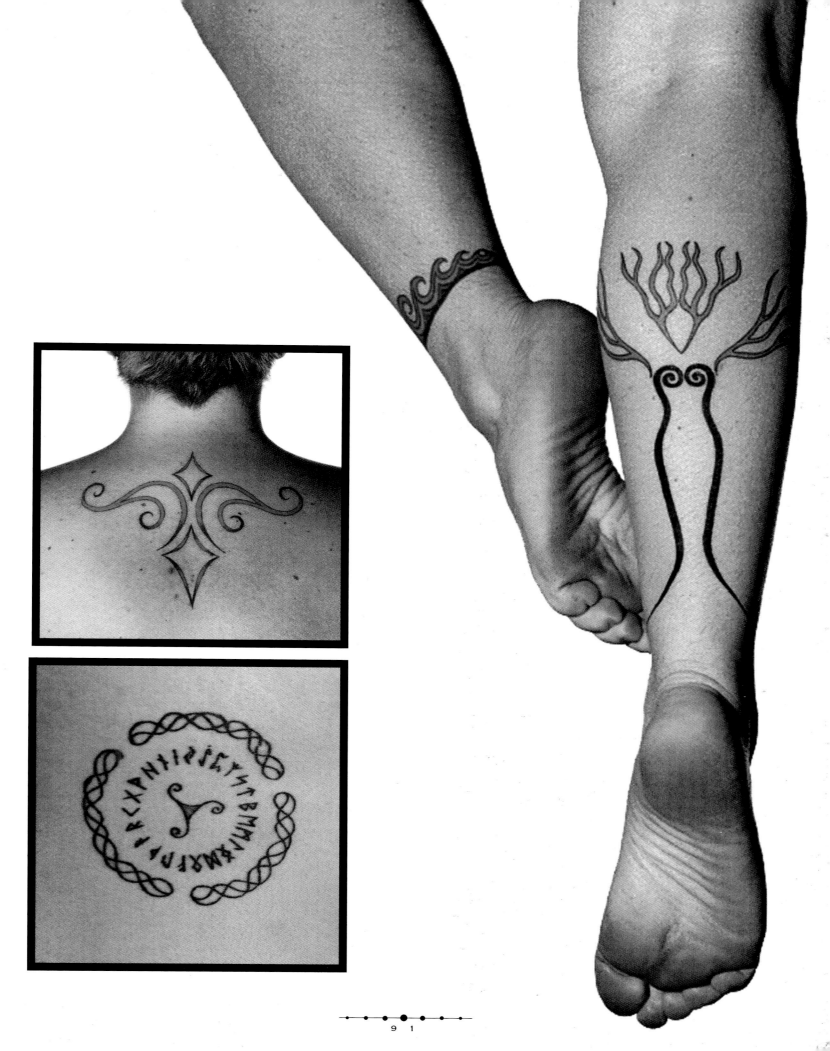

I love the imagery of the corset and the
feeling of restriction when wearing
it. Before I started cross-
dressing, I
used to wear a
very tight belt around my
waist. My ideal size would be 24
inches — my natural waist is around 28 inches.

PAULA, PROJECT MANAGER, 42

The corset is one of the
most comforting things to wear.
It holds you so tight, it's like
a really firm hug. It's
an aggressive,
hard
femininity,
an armour. I like the
extremity of what a corset
can do — you can make the most
ridiculous shape out of your body.
I see my body as a work in progress.
I like to see what I can do to it, to temper it.

FELINA, 28

PHOTOS: PAUL OVENDEN, AUSTRALIAN MUSEUM

PHOTO: PAUL OVENDEN, AUSTRALIAN MUSEUM

I like to subvert expectations and the feminine ideal. By putting on these things which are traditionally considered restricting and then recontextualising them from a position of power, I feel like I am making a point about women's bodies and power. Besides, corsetry gives me great posture.

ANNE DUNN, CONSULTANT, 27

AMAZING BODY ART FACTS

"THERESE" REDUCED THE SIZE OF HER WAIST TO BELOW 20 INCHES PRIMARILY BY WEARING A CORSET

"BULELWA", AN INDIGENOUS SOUTH AFRICAN WOMAN, HAS RAZOR BLADE SCARS BEHIND HER EARS. HER XHOSA TRIBE BELIEVE THESE MARKS WILL PROTECT HER FROM BAD SPIRITS.

"PIERCER PAUL" HAS 100 GENITAL PIERCINGS. HE HAS ANOTHER 57 PIERCINGS ON OTHER PARTS OF HIS BODY.

BIKER "ARM" HAS TATTOOED HIS FULL BODY, INCLUDING A TRADITIONAL SAMOAN LEG TATTOO AND HUNDREDS OF CONTEMPORARY DESIGNS.

PRINCE ALBERT PENIS PIERCINGS ARE NAMED AFTER QUEEN VICTORIA'S HUSBAND. IT IS THOUGHT THAT HE WAS ALREADY PIERCED BEFORE HIS MARRIAGE TO THE QUEEN IN 1825. THESE PIERCINGS ALLOWED THE PENIS TO BE HOOKED TO ONE SIDE WHEN WEARING THE TIGHT TROUSERS THAT WERE FASHIONABLE AT THE TIME.

"In all ages, far back into prehistory, we find human beings have painted and adorned themselves."

HG Wells